HOW TO AVOID BEING MISLED BY STATISTICS.

I0493967

Don't Be One of the 60% Who are Below Average.

INTRODUCTION.

Three kinds of people ought to read this book.

Firstly there are those who use statistics in their work: accountants, scientists, advertisers, marketers, politicians and journalists. If you are in one of these categories I would like to help you to maintain, or aspire to, a reasonable standard of honesty and integrity, so that people can trust what you say, and so that you do not even inadvertently mislead yourself as well as others.

Secondly there are cynics who think statistics can never be trusted and are just tools used by liars. I want to show that they can be used properly, and also that with a little thought, we can all learn to spot the false or exaggerated claims, the non-sequiturs, and the unsubstantiated assumptions. Then we will be able to see the truth when it appears.

Thirdly, there are the huge number of ordinary people who get totally confused and sometimes, sadly, misled, by statistics. I want to help you make sense of what you read or hear, and to be able to be confident in sorting the facts from the hype.

It is for this third group that this book is really written. If the other two groups benefit, I will be glad, but if you are in this third group, please read on. I hope you will enjoy it, but above all I hope it will empower you.

AUTHOR'S NOTE

If you find nothing new here, do not be surprised. Most of the mistakes and tricks in the use of statistics have been around for a long time, and have probably been pointed out by previous writers, but you might be one of the many people who are still not aware of them, so I think it is time to enlighten you. When the producers and users of statistics start making new mistakes or invent some new tricks, I will have to write a sequel to this book.

"If a man will begin in certainties, he shall end in doubts; but if he will be content to begin with doubts he shall end in certainties." – Francis Bacon.

CHAPTER I

Can I Help You To Trust Statistics?

In my career in Accountancy, Insurance and Risk Management I have had to use statistics a lot. This is something those of us in such areas of management have in common with people involved in medical and other types of scientific research. Unfortunately, however, we are also in the company of politicians, journalists and salesmen: groups generally regarded, rightly or wrongly, as untrustworthy. That is probably why so many people do not trust statistics.

Now, there are two reasons why I tend to be sceptical of statistics or anything else, until I have good reason to believe them.

- Firstly, I am not a very trusting person in my nature. My patron saint is really St. John the Evangelist but some people think it should be St. Thomas the Doubter. Well, that is fair enough, because, like Thomas, I am usually sceptical, but am open to being convinced by reason and evidence. (Remember that Thomas eventually believed in the Resurrection when he had seen the risen Christ with his own eyes).
- Secondly, I have spent many years in Internal Audit and also many years dealing with liability claims. I have come across plenty of frauds, scams, and dishonest claims. Wherever there is an opportunity to make a dishonest penny, or several, there is always someone there to make the most of it. If every claim I have seen for tripping on the pavement was true, you ought to see someone fall down nearly every time you go out!

However, I do not distrust statistics in particular. Dishonest people use anything they can: facts, words, pictures, and quotes from the Bible. There are also many people who use statistics lazily and mislead others without intending to be dishonest, because they do not think clearly about what they really mean, or they have misled themselves into jumping to conclusions which the facts do not really support.

Yet all these things can be used rightly and in a way that informs rather than misleads. The Victorian Prime Minister, Benjamin Disraeli is supposed to have said there were *"Lies, damned lies and statistics"*, but the writer Andrew Lang said of someone *"he uses statistics as a drunken man uses a lamp-post: for support rather than illumination"*, thus blaming the user rather than the "lamp-post". Well, I want us all to gain illumination as we use statistics in whatever field. They can help us to:

- establish facts
- reduce guesswork
- gain a sense of proportion
- identify the most important issues
- find what works and what does not.

Fortunately, we can avoid being misled when we know about a number of giveaways which I learned about a long time ago and have always found very useful. So in this book I am going to show **how** statistics can be, and often are, misused, so as to put you on your guard and enable you to sift the truth from the lies, and especially from the half-truths, and to help you avoid inadvertently misleading yourself and others.

"A wise scepticism is the first attribute of a good critic." – James Russell Lowell.

CHAPTER II

Much Ado About (Almost) Nothing!

Here is one popular misuse of statistics I see all the time. This is to exaggerate the importance of a minor change in something or a small difference between two things. This is often done by journalists trying to create a story out of a factual report which does not actually reveal anything very exciting. To build it up into a story, the journalist usually leaves out a lot of the statistical information or presents it in such a manner as to draw attention to the selected element only.

There are two ways this can be done.

The first way is to report on a large percentage change, or difference, without pointing out the absolute size of the figures.
- If a new medical treatment or "healthy diet" reduces your chances of developing a certain disease by 25% it sounds worth trying, even if it costs a lot of money. Unless you know that your original chances of getting the disease were only 1 in 40 million, meaning the improved treatment or diet reduced it to 1 in 30 million. So what?
- If a the number of cases of a certain type of crime in England and Wales has increased by 50% it sounds as if something must be done and soon. Unless you know that the average number for several years was 10 crimes a year, and last year there were 15. Is this something to worry about?

The second way is almost the opposite. It is to emphasise the absolute numbers without mentioning the percentages.
- If 100 people have complained about a product it sounds pretty bad. Unless you know that 100,000 people bought the product last year, so only 0.1% had anything to complain about.
- If an additional 20 people were killed in industrial accidents last year, you might think we were losing our obsession with Health & Safety, if you did not know that the total number killed in any year was several hundred.

So always look at both the percentage differences **and** the absolute numbers before deciding it is time to shout "don't panic!" or to demand "action".

[N.B. All figures stated above are made up for purely illustrative purposes.]

"Things are seldom what they seem, skim milk masquerades as cream." – W.S.Gilbert, HMS Pinafore.

CHAPTER III

A Picture Can Tell a Thousand Lies.

Statistics are often presented with pictures or graphs, supposedly because this makes them easier to understand, but this opens up another opportunity for misleading the reader, either deliberately or accidentally. Suppose you want to show that last year's sales, or whatever, were 1000 and this year's are 2000. The simplest and most honest way of illustrating it is to draw a picture of a money-bag or piggy-bank and then two bags or pigs, the same size. The deception occurs if you try illustrating the bigger figures with a bigger picture, such as a piggy-bank twice as big as the first.

Year 1   **Year 2**

This is because if you double all the dimensions, the total area the picture takes up is increased four times, not twice, and that is how the eye, and therefore the brain, reads it. You could try increasing only the height or only the width to keep the overall area in its correct proportion but that does tend to look silly. It is better to just show two pigs or whatever.

Year 1   **Year 2**

Graphs and charts can also be misleading.

They can be flattened or steepened by adjusting the scale on one of the axes to make a small variation look significant. If sales had gone up from 1000 to 1010 it should look like the minor change it is, but it could look like a big jump if you make the figures appear to start at 900 rather than showing the relevant axis, usually the vertical one, to start at zero. I notice that a lot of graphs functions automatically adjust the axes to emphasise small changes, presumably to save space and to make them seem clearer, but they do tend to mislead unless you mentally adjust the other way.

Here are two ways of making a small increase in sales over four years seem like a big increase. Firstly in a bar chart, secondly in a line graph.

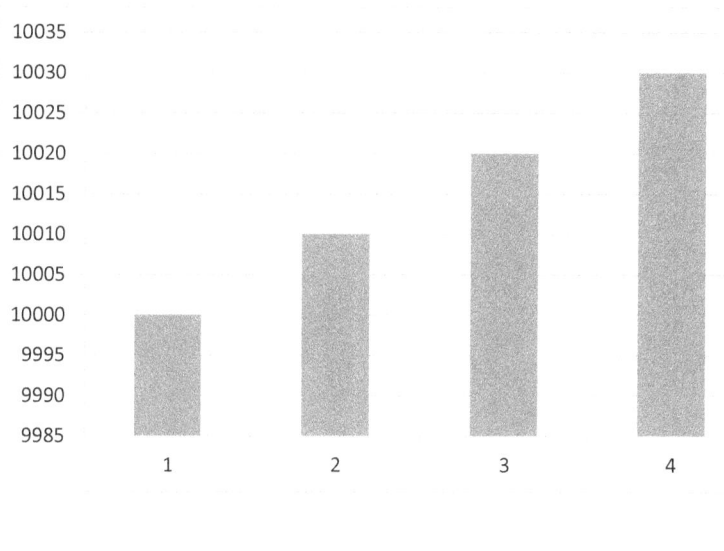

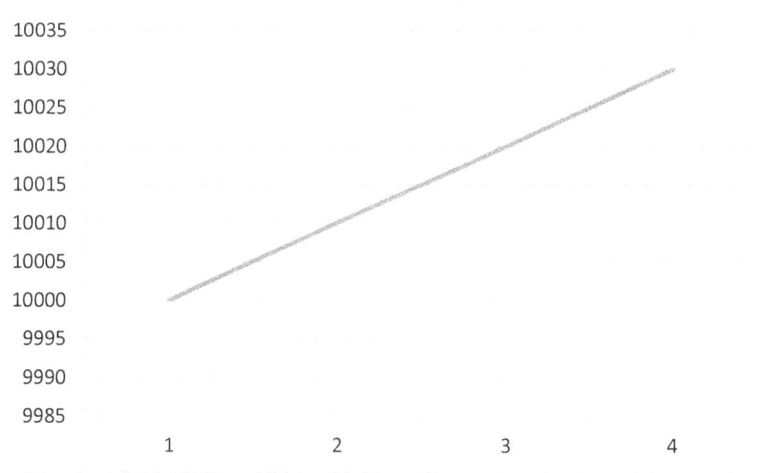

Now here is an example of a graph that does not distort in that way, showing values of, say, the number of crimes in each of the last 10 years.

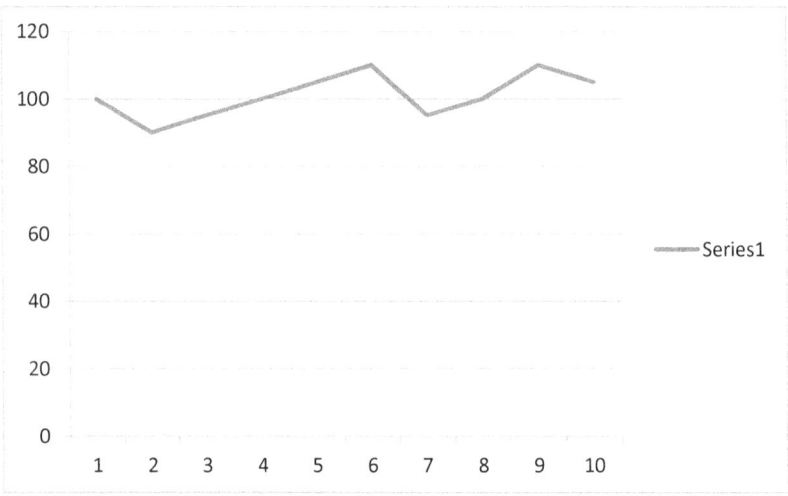

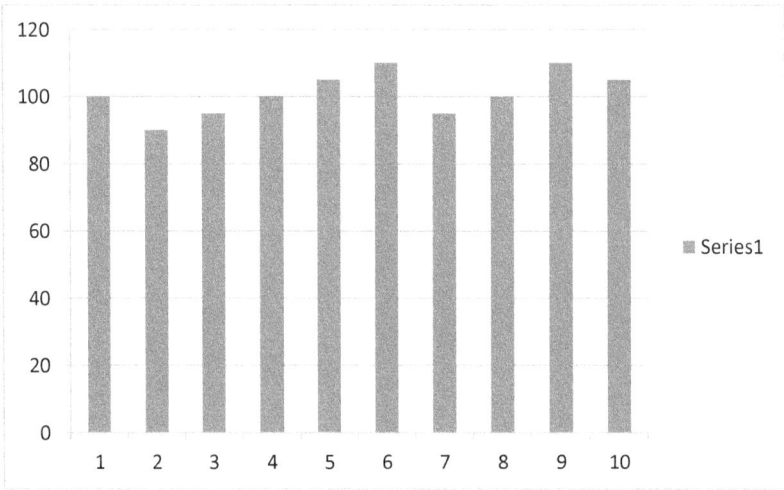

These could be made to look more dramatic but also misleading, if only a few years were chosen, to give the impression of a steady or even rapid increase or decrease, when in fact the situation is fairly static with annual fluctuations. Never look at a graph without looking at the actual figures and asking what they really tell you.

"You should say what you mean." Said the March Hare.

"I do." Hastily replied Alice. "At least I mean what I say - that's the same thing, you know."

 - Lewis Carroll, Alice in Wonderland.

CHAPTER IV

Are You One of The 60% Who Are Below Average?

Many people find statistics confusing for many reasons, not least because of the ways in which they are often presented, as we have seen. To all this there is often added the confusion of the meaning of the terms used, and none is more commonly misunderstood than the word "average". The word is used in everyday speech to cover three distinct mathematical concepts, each of which has its uses. Often it is all right as we do not always need to be precise, but when reporting on statistics people really should be clear as to what they are saying.

I will use a simple, made-up, example, which I hope will illustrate my point. Consider this series of values. Let's say each represents the value of sales for a different business for a particular month. It does not matter whether they are in pounds, thousands or millions – unless one of them is your business!

Company.	Sales.
A	20
B	25
C	25
D	30
E	35
F	50
G	50
H	50
I	75
Total	360

The Mean is the simple average obtained by adding all the values in a series and dividing by the number of items. In this case 360 divided by 9 making 40.

The Median is the middle value, which will have as many above it as below. As these are set out in ascending order the median will be the middle i.e. company E, the fifth in the list, with a value of 35.

The Mode is the most commonly occurring value. The most "typical" result. In this case it is easy to see that value is 50.

Think where you would mark each of the three averages on this graph.

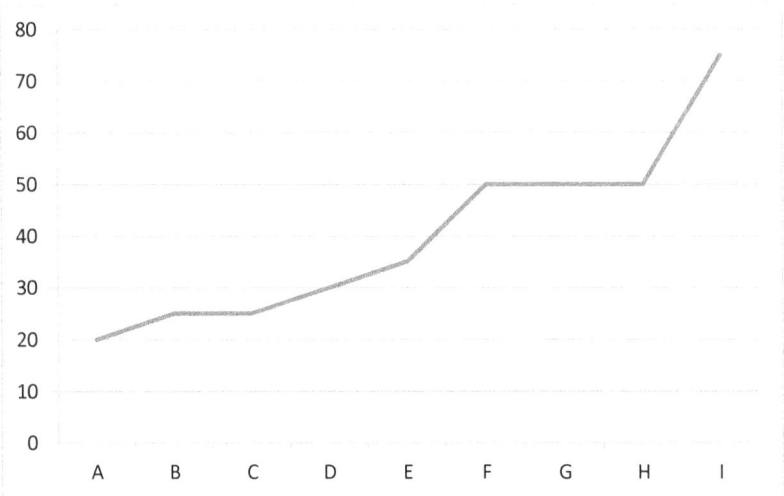

In many cases the three averages are the same, as a lot of things seem to cluster around the middle, but as the above example illustrates, they can be very different. So you could easily find that the majority of people were below the median and/or the mode, as is the case in real life if we look at incomes, although obviously only half of us will ever be below, or above, the mean.

"Theirs not to reason why." – Tennyson, The Charge of the Light Brigade.

CHAPTER V

Ask a Silly Question.

Another way to mislead with statistics is to weight the question you ask, or to target groups of people who are likely to answer it in a certain way. Then make the predictable results sound like an amazing discovery.

I could predict the following without holding an opinion poll:

- The majority of unemployed people think unemployment is too high.
- The majority of taxpayers think taxes are too high.
- The majority of victims of crime think sentencing is too lenient.
- The majority of people convicted of offences think sentencing is too severe.
- The majority of farmers do not want farm subsidies to be scrapped.

You will rarely see these pairs of questions asked in the same survey, or if so I suspect the answers to only one of each pair would be published:

1. a. Would you like to see immigration reduced?

1. b. Would you like the NHS to stop recruiting foreign doctors and nurses?

2. a. How long do you think terrorists should be detained without trial?

2. b. What is the definition of a terrorist?

3. a. Should there be stiffer penalties for tax evasion?

3. b. Do you ever pay tradesmen cash-in-hand?

4. a. Should more money be spent on X?

4. b. Should less money be spent on Y?

4. c. Should Council Tax be capped?

5. a. Should local authorities have more power to respond to local needs?

5. b. Should something be done about the postcode lottery?

I would also expect this same basic question to get a different answer if it was asked in each of these different ways:

1. Should businesses be subject to less state interference?
2. Should more be done to ensure adequate standards of consumer protection/safety/transparency?

Or similarly:

1. Do we need to do more to protect the countryside?
2. Should there be fewer planning restrictions?

So what I am saying is that you should always check what questions have actually been asked, and what groups of people were selected. If that information is not given, be very suspicious!

"Mathematics possesses not only truth, but supreme beauty – a beauty cold and austere, like that of sculpture." – Bertrand Russell.

CHAPTER VI

The Confusion of Multiple Connections!

I want to expand on a point I have made briefly in some other chapters, which is that many things we try to study are more complex than some people would have us believe.

The obvious thing that many people seem to overlook is that human behaviour, whether as individuals or groups, is influenced by many factors. Not only that, but most of the factors affect each other too. So trying to isolate one factor or one relationship takes a lot of skill and effort and the results still need approaching with caution.

When thinking about social phenomena, most people are aware that how we behave and how successful we are in whatever we do is influenced by, among other things, our health, education, wealth, social standing and ethnicity. However, it is all too easy to forget that each of these is affected by the others, and that these things often work in both directions.

It is too simplistic to say, for instance, that unemployment has harmful effects on people's health, and to try to prove it by showing statistical relationships between areas of high unemployment and areas where certain mental or physical ailments are prevalent. The complication is that being in poor health makes it harder to get a job. It also makes you less likely to succeed in work, if you do find any.

In the same way, poor education can be shown to be either a cause or an effect of poverty, or of poor health. The better off your parents are, the better you are likely to perform in school, but academic success can obviously help you get a job and succeed in your career. Ill health can cause you to miss some of your schooling or to not be up to concentrating enough to pass your exams.

Higher rates of poverty among ethnic minorities can all too easily be used as evidence that they suffer discrimination. Now, I am not saying that discrimination does not occur, but I am saying that other factors come into it too. Language is one factor. Everyone accepts that the inability to speak English is a barrier to employment in the U.K. but not everyone appreciates the extent to which your career can suffer just because English is your second language even if you are pretty fluent.

I once met a Chinese woman who had lived here a long time and seemed very fluent. However, one day her boss was reprimanding her for something and ended with the words "and you had better pull your socks up!" to which she replied "but I am not wearing any". This left both of them feeling aggrieved: he because he thought she was being cheeky, she because she really did not know that we use the term "pull your socks up" metaphorically. A few incidents like that would not do your career much good.

The same issue occurs when we look at medical research. An example of inadvertent misuse of statistics can be found in some of the reactions to a report a few years ago into the increase in cases of rickets. It was noted that most of the new cases were in black or Asian people in the North of England. Some commentators tried to make some sort of social comment about poverty and/or the failings of the NHS.

The truth is that rickets is caused by a deficiency in vitamin A and lack of exposure to sunlight is a major factor. People with dark skin do not process sunlight into vitamin A as well as pale-skinned people. The NHS is not to blame for the lack of sunlight in the North of England. One cultural factor which probably adds to the problem, is that many Asians are reluctant to expose their skin to direct sunlight due to their sense of modesty, so they do not make the most of what little sunshine there is around here.

The study of climate change has also been clouded with the interrelations between multiple factors. We can certainly see from statistics that the long-term trend seems to be that the world is getting warmer, but isolating the cause has proved difficult and controversial. In particular, statistics cannot really answer the question of whether human activity is the sole or even principal cause. As to identifying which activity, or activities, to blame, there seems little chance of establishing the answer to that question with any degree of certainty.

Personally, I think we should be putting more effort into preparing for the probable results of climate change, and less into studying its causes. However, I recognise that many of the actions proposed in order to reduce global warming are desirable for other reasons. Being more fuel-efficient, reducing reliance on fossil fuels, and improving recycling of all kinds of products are all things we should aim at for many good reasons, whereas producing arguments from statistics as to the links between industrial activity and global warming seems to me to be futile.

Although we could go into issues of cultural awareness, language teaching, the NHS, climate change and a lot more, my main point is that an overly simplistic interpretation of statistics tends to ignore the many complexities of the relationships between various social and economic factors affecting our lives.

Produce statistics, yes. Use them, by all means. But please ask lots of questions about what lies behind them. (No lies at all, I hope!)

"Comment is free but facts are sacred." –
C.P.Scott, the Manchester Guardian.

CHAPTER VII

How Reliable are the "Facts" Anyway?

There is an old saying in the world of computer programming: GIGO, which stands for "Garbage In, Garbage Out". This applies in many other areas of life, and certainly to the use of statistics. If you start with wrong information you will end with wrong conclusions. Simple! The essential first step in the process of producing statistics is often called "data capture" which means getting hold of the basic information. But how often do we ask about the way that step was carried out when we look at statistics?

Think about the times you provide that basic information for someone, such as when you answer a questionnaire, whether on paper or online, or even when you are stopped in the street by someone doing market research:

- How clear are the questions? (There is an art, or science, in producing questionnaires, but it is not always practiced).
- How much time or effort do you put into your answers?
- Do you often find yourself mentally tossing a coin to decide whether you were "totally satisfied" or "quite satisfied" with a product, or whether you do something "often" or "sometimes"?
- What do you do when asked a question you would rather not answer? Perhaps about your income or health. You might even want to keep your opinions on certain things private if you are unsure how anonymous or confidential your answers will be, especially when the questions are being asked on behalf of your employer or the Government. Do you ever give in to the temptation to give a safe, bland answer or leave that one blank?
- What assumptions do you think the statisticians will make about the blanks? Or the "don't knows"?

Sometimes researchers do not have to rely on the answers you or I give. They can get the information they need by counting the number of people using a facility, or the number of cars using a road, or the number of badgers living in a wood. Can we rely on these sorts of things being measured more accurately?

The front-line research is not always carried out by the scientists or others studying the phenomena in question. They often use students, volunteers, or casual employees to do a lot of it for them. This raises some more questions for us:

- How committed are these data-collectors to the project?
- How much training do they get to ensure consistency?
- Do they have to use initiative to interpret what they see? E.g. do they include people who came and went without really using the facility? Is a motorcycle with a sidecar a vehicle? Is that the same badger or another?

Another factor which has often, but not often enough, been recognised as reducing the reliability of statistics is under-reporting. This is especially true when we are studying crimes, accidents, and certain diseases. People do not always bother reporting such things unless they think it is worthwhile. So if there is a widespread belief that the police or other relevant authorities, are not likely to take any effective action, a lot will go unreported.

The problem for anyone trying to interpret the resulting statistics is not only to estimate the proportion of incidents which are not reported, but also to guess whether that proportion has remained constant throughout the period under scrutiny. It is even worse if there is the possibility of different levels of under-reporting in different areas. That could happen if, for instance, one police-force had a better reputation than another and so the better force appeared to be performing less well because people were more willing to report crimes!

We have to use statistics to understand the sorts of phenomena mentioned, but unless we have satisfactory answers to the sort of questions above, we should take the conclusions with a pinch of salt. Or more than a pinch perhaps.

P.S. I have just heard someone making some very bold claims about the opinions of the majority of people in the UK based on a survey of 1000 people. How typical were they? Out of over 60 million – yes, million – Britons!

"No man will be a sailor if he has contrivance enough to get himself into a jail; for being on a ship is being in a jail with the chance of being drowned. A man in jail has more room, better food and commonly better company." - Dr. Samuel Johnson.

CHAPTER VIII

How The US Navy Fooled Themselves With Statistics.

Here is an example of an accidental deception on a large scale due to misinterpreting statistics.

In the early 20th Century the US Navy discovered that the death rate among its sailors was lower than that in the American population in general. This information was used in their recruiting publicity. Most people believed that this was because sailors led a healthier lifestyle and got better food and medical care than the average person.

After some time, somebody spoilt the party by pointing out that the fair comparison would be between the death rate in the Navy and that of men aged from their late teens to early thirties. The senior officers in the Navy, as well as a lot of other people, were shocked when they found that the death rate in the Navy was actually much higher than that among other men in that age-group. In the general population, of course, many people died of old age, infant and childhood diseases and complications around childbirth, which facts made the original oversimplified comparison utterly misleading.

This shows how easy it is to be deceived by statistics, or even to deceive yourself, by simply failing to ask whether you are really comparing like with like. I have no reason to think that anyone in the US Navy was being deliberately dishonest, and I am sure many people today jump to conclusions without asking the right questions. So just think how often we are all likely to be misled by advertisers, politicians and journalists who **do** want to mislead us! Think about some of these examples:

- If brushing your teeth with ABC reduces decay by x% is that compared with other brands or with not brushing them at all?
- If children at a certain school perform better at GCSE than the national average, is it because of something they are doing at the school, or because it is in an area where most parents are well-off and ambitious for their children?
- If a poll shows that x% of the readers of a certain newspaper agree with something, is it because that paper attracts a certain type of person?
- If another poll shows y% of people are dissatisfied with the Government/the Council/the BBC, is it because the dissatisfied ones are more likely to respond to the poll than anyone else?

So always ask whether the two things being compared are truly comparable, and what other factors might be influencing one or both of them.

"I can trace my ancestry back to a proplasmal primordial atomic globule. Consequently, my family pride is something inconceivable. I can't help it. I was born sneering." – W.S.Gilbert, the Mikado.

CHAPTER IX

Whether Your Ancestors were Toffs or Plebs, You will be Amazed to Find How Closely Related We are.

In this chapter we will look at an example of statistics helping us to see a truth which would not appear obvious to most of us, just to remind ourselves that not everyone uses them to mislead.

If class means anything more than money, most people think it must be connected to heredity: your ancestry determines who you are. However, by applying simple arithmetic to basic biology, it is likely that you will find you have far more relatives than you imagined, and they must be spread across all classes. I hope this climb up your family tree will be fruitful, and not just lead to a bunch of nuts!

If you have ever looked up your ancestry, unless you have been uncommonly thorough or lucky, you will probably have not tried to go back more than a century or two, and will have only followed one or two branches, leaving most of the tree unexplored. What about the big picture? As the conclusion is likely to surprise you, I want to take us one step at a time.

Begin where we are.

Lets start with the basics, so we can all agree about something.

Everybody has two parents, even if we don't know who they are – right? Well, they might not still be alive, so I should say everybody has *had* two parents. Therefore we have all got, or, had four grandparents, eight great grandparents and so on, doubling the number for each generation.

So you could draw up a family tree with double the number of branches for each generation, putting names and dates on as many as you could, then filling in the rest with names like A.N.Other and reasonable guesses at dates. It is often assumed that 25 years is a fair average for the difference in birthdates between parents and children, where there is nothing better to go on.

I have worked out that I must have had 16 great-great grandparents alive in 1850, whoever they were.

Now for the Big Picture.

Assuming myself to be average (not a term many people would use to describe me) and supposing everybody in Britain carried out this exercise, we would end up with 61 million trees with 16 branches each, making a total of 976 million branches representing 976 million individuals, as there are 61 million people in Britain today, as per the 2011 census. [You might want to include another 7 million for the population of Ireland as so many of us have at least one Irish grandparent. You might also want to remove about 8 or 9 million for those living in Britain today who were born, or whose parents or grandparents were born overseas, as I expect most of them will not be closely related to the rest of us. We end up with a figure not far from 60 million anyway.]

But there are too many! How is that possible?

You will not be surprised to learn that the population of Britain in 1850 was a lot less than 976 million. In fact the 1851 census gave a total population of just 20 million. This means that a lot of us must have several ancestors in common. Unless each of us has on average 48 brothers and sisters, or 96 first cousins, we must all have hundreds of second or third cousins. If you are certain that you do not, then someone else must have twice as many to offset it. (I think if I went into this thoroughly I would have to buy a lot more Christmas cards.)

Taking it further

Working back up my family tree on this basis, I calculate that I would have had:

- 64 ancestors alive in 1800, when the population was only 8 million
- 1024 in 1700 when the population was about 5 or 6 million
- 16,384 in 1600 when the population was about 4 or 5 million
- 258,000 in 1500 when the population was about 4 million

In other words, my ancestors, or anyone else's, made up about a sixteenth of the country, meaning that every time over 16 people come together today, some of them must have common ancestors going back to 1500.

If you found that hard to take in, this is where it becomes impossible!

The real shock comes when we go back to 1400. Each of us must have had over four million ancestors alive in 1400 but the population was only about three and a half million and not all of them became anyone's ancestors – those who died young, those who were infertile, those in holy orders and others who chose not to have children. So I, and every one of us, must have a lot of the same ancestors several times over, as well as having most of my ancestors in common with most other people in Britain today. Then, if you go back further, it gets even more amazing, with ancestors outnumbering the population several times over, making it even less likely that we are not related.

What does all this mean?

So what? Well, if you think your family are different from the rest of us, whether aristocrats, followers of a certain trade, or even something at the bottom end of Society, think again! Perhaps you do know that your father, grandfather, great grandfather, etc. etc. were all tinkers, tailors, soldiers, or sailors, but what about your grandmothers' ancestors and all the others?

Even if you are an earl and can trace your ancestry to an earl in, say, 1500, he was only one of 258,000 ancestors you had in 1500 and there were not 258,000 earls. In fact, back then there were probably only about a thousand or perhaps two thousand noblemen of all kinds – dukes, barons, knights and earls – including Scottish and Irish nobles. Therefore, the vast majority of your ancestors must have been, well... common! On the other hand if you think you are a "nobody", you are just as wrong. You are probably related to some of the most important families in Britain.

If you are sceptical, feel free to check all my facts and figures and re-do this exercise using your own, but I am sure you will find the conclusions will be the same.

"I'm not denyin' that women are foolish: God Almighty made 'em to match the men." – George Eliot, a woman who used a male pen-name to get round the prejudices of publishers and readers.

CHAPTER X

How Statistics Have Helped Women.

If any group of people should be grateful for statistics being used correctly, that group is women!

On the Road.

I can remember a time when very few women drove cars, and very few drivers were women. You did not need to look at any statistics to notice that. In those days most men thought women were definitely inferior to men as drivers, whatever else they might be good at. Insurance companies accepted this as received wisdom, and charged women higher premiums than men. Nearly all comedians had a stock list of woman-driver jokes, generally about women being easily distracted by such trivia as sales adverts in shop windows, not knowing right from left, and thinking the car's mirror was for checking their make-up. Some men thought that allowing women to drive was even more irresponsible than giving them the vote. Ironically, one woman who did not drive was especially unpopular with most male motorists: the Minister of Transport in the mid-1960's, Barbara Castle.

On the Buses.

The cause of women's equality was not helped by an unfortunate and highly publicised incident. There was a bus-conductress in Yorkshire, Bradford I think. (For the benefit of younger readers, I had better explain that a bus-conductor, or if female conductress, was someone who collected fares, issued tickets and maintained order on busses. Nowadays bus-drivers are expected to do all the foregoing duties as well as driving the vehicle. The change was made in the name of efficiency.) This woman was determined to become a bus-driver, and managed to get her employers to give her all the necessary training. There was then a lot of controversy as most of her male colleagues objected, putting management in a dilemma. After much debate, they let her drive. She then had three accidents in the first three days she was on the road. Whether this was due to her lack of ability, to the stress she was under with all the controversy, or just bad luck, I do not know. I do know that this single example was quoted frequently, as if conclusive proof that women should not be allowed to drive. You will observe that a single incident, or three, hardly counts as significant statistically.

The Heroes.

Eventually women's self-esteem was rescued, making the comedians seek other targets, by an unlikely band of champions: insurance underwriters! These unsung heroes actually knew how to collect, analyse and interpret statistics correctly. They discovered the fact that women generally had fewer accidents than men. This information led to lower premiums being charged to women-drivers, to the amazement of most men. I will not speculate as to the reasons for this difference, I merely state a fact.

Through the Ceiling?

Statistics have also helped the broader movement for women's equality, by providing factual information as to the numbers of women employed in various organisations, and their levels of pay. This has provided almost conclusive proof of the existence of the "glass ceiling" in many occupations, as well as of the unequal pay for the same or similar work in certain industries. This information has not always led to the immediate rectification of the injustices, but it has at least forced Society to face the facts and stop being in denial.

What About Multiple Connections?

You may think I have just contradicted something I said in an earlier chapter about multiple factors influencing human behaviour. I acknowledge that there may be causes other than discrimination to explain some of the apparent inequalities, such as women choosing to avoid certain occupations, or disabilities genuinely preventing some people doing certain jobs. However, the statistical evidence has forced employers to accept that there is a case to answer, and that it must be answered properly, not with unsubstantiated excuses.

And Finally

Although I stand by my warnings about the many ways you can be misled by statistics, I want to remind you of the value of statistics when they are used properly. I hope you can see that statistics can and should be used to illuminate and inform rather than to do the very opposite as they so often do. So be on your guard, be aware and mentally adjust for the biases and distortions you may come across. And please, please, if you ever produce a report or statement using statistics, whether from your own research or someone else's, do try very hard to avoid accidentally misleading others by your own sloppy thinking or poor presentation.

Be empowered!

JOHN HARVEY MURRAY

After studying Economics and Accountancy at Bristol University, John worked in accountancy and audit in several types of local authority prior to becoming Insurance Officer at St Helens Council where he achieved considerable savings in the cost of insurance and risk, which results compared favourably with those of other authorities, according to independent sources. This was achieved by improving claims-handling and risk management as well as by restructuring the insurance programme. John also made changes to the Council's insurance tendering process in order to obtain the best value for the money spent on premiums.

He is currently self-employed as JHM Risk Management Services, offering risk management and liability claims-handling services to businesses and other organisations, to enable owners and managers to save time and stress as well as money. John is a member of the accountancy body CIPFA, is a Registered Risk Practitioner with ALARM, and is a Specialist Member of the Institute of Risk Managers.

John now offers data-protection both as stand-alone and as part of an integrated risk management service, and can help clients deal with claims arising from data breaches as well as from other sources.

www.jhmriskmanagementservices.co.uk

www.ingramcontent.com/pod-product-compliance
Lightning Source LLC
Chambersburg PA
CBHW070718180526
45167CB00004B/1530

9781499190489